Defamers

Table of Contents

Foreward

Anyone who follows news and commentary about the Arab-Israeli conflict knows that Jewish voices raised against Israel—often stridently and inaccurately—are commonplace. They are welcomed in the opinion columns of America's most influential newspapers, in the pages of prestigious magazines and journals and on many airwaves. No one doubts the right of such Jewish critics to denounce the Jewish state—just as others are entitled to challenge their allegations and consider the aims and consequences of their at times extensively publicized attacks.

On October 21, 2007 in New York City, CAMERA convened a conference to begin exploring the issue of Israel's Jewish Defamers and to encourage open discussion of their disquieting role in both American and international discourse about the Jewish state, its history, conduct and future.

The capacity crowd in attendance at the event underscored the strong interest in this important subject and encouraged us to publish the speakers' presentations for distribution to a wider audience. We hope this monograph adds to an understanding of the need for still further discussion of a dimension of the debate about Israel that is too often misunderstood—and ignored.

Andrea Levin
Executive Director, CAMERA
July 2008

Israel's *Ha'aretz* Newspaper: The Global Impact of Local Bias

by Andrea Levin

Good afternoon and welcome to a conference whose time has more than come.

We at CAMERA—the Committee for Accuracy in Middle East Reporting in America—have long encountered the daunting challenge of self-identified Jewish figures being given prominent news media platforms to defame Israel with totally baseless, extreme and propagandistic charges.

We emphasize the word defame. We mean defame—we don't mean criticize. The word was considered carefully in arranging this event and we urge reporters and others here today to note this.

None of this discussion concerns the reasonable and undeniably legitimate right of Jews or anyone else to fault Israel for an action or political choice. Anyone following the subject of the Middle East knows Israel's history, policies, military actions—all aspects of the nation's existence—are scrutinized and debated. While much of this criticism may be out of proportion to scrutiny given other nations and objectionable on those grounds—what we are addressing today is criticism rooted in outright, demonstrable falsehood or wildly extreme, out-of-context distortion.

In an era of increasing demonization of Israel and the Jewish people, we are compelled to address the singular role of Jews—some of them famous and celebrated—whose excoriations of Israel are divorced from factual reality and whose voluble denigrations of Israel echo and fuel the most extreme attacks, including those leveled by groups calling for the elimination of the Jewish state.

What we are addressing with regard to *Ha'aretz* is criticism rooted in outright, demonstrable falsehood or wildly extreme, out-of-context distortion.

Because of the enormous damage being done by such defamers, we are compelled not to ignore this difficult subject. And just as we would challenge defamatory falsehoods and distortions by any other commentators, we challenge those of Jewish writers, reporters and celebrities who use their ethnic background for added potency in delivering distorted and mendacious allegations against Israel and the Jews—often explicitly invoking their heritage as testament to the merit of their statements.

So let us consider what is being said and by whom and—even—why. And, very importantly, what we can do.

My own focus this afternoon is the role of the Israeli newspaper *Ha'aretz*—and I begin with another caveat. We believe Amos Shocken, the third generation in his family to publish the paper, and a substantial number of *Ha'aretz* writers, some of whom I'll mention, are manifestly reckless and indifferent to fact in reporting realities in Israel, the West Bank, Gaza and beyond, and cause immeasurable, unwarranted misunderstanding of and enmity toward Israel. However, we hasten to say there are fine, conscientious, professional journalists at the paper as well. Some of Israel's very best.

Their writing may often include information unflattering to Israel, but it's accurate, fair and in context. And there's no complaint from us. Once more, fair and accurate criticism is not the subject of our discussion.

A quick bit of background: *Ha'aretz,* which means "The Land" in Hebrew, was founded in 1919 and was until recently a relatively low-circulation Hebrew language paper of the left with influence in Israeli academic, political and cultural circles. Its audience and influence increased substantially with the appearance of its English-language version in 1997 as part of a joint venture with the *International Herald Tribune,* reaching a daily distribution of roughly 100,000 for the Hebrew and English editions combined. The foreign press and diplomatic corps at that point had ready access to its content.

Today, it enjoys even greater influence with a global reach to millions via the paper's popular Web site.

Ironically, a former editor-in-chief, Hanoch Marmari—who was replaced in 2004 by David Landau—expressed awareness of this global impact in a candid address to an international media conference in May 2002. He deplored what he called "fundamental sins" of international media coverage generally of the Palestinian-Israeli crisis, including "obsessiveness, prejudice, condescension and ignorance." And he added a fifth pertaining to Israeli media. For papers like *Ha'aretz,* prone to exposés of alleged Israeli wrongdoing published in the belief "that our work helps clean the system," Marmari cited as well "the sin of naivete."

He observed that a story castigating Israel and carrying the "brand name" of *Ha'aretz* can appear to offer, in his words, "proof of Israel's profound and pervasive evil."

Yes, indeed. Check the Internet and you'll find rosters of columns by *Ha'aretz* writers listed on some of the most virulent anti-Israel and anti-Jewish sites. They are undoubtedly included with relish as perfect validation for the views of these detractors. Some of the most extreme *Ha'aretz* writers are also championed in more elevated venues in Great Britain and the rest of Europe, and given prizes, quoted in the media and invited to elite conferences.

A story castigating Israel and carrying the "brand name" of *Ha'aretz* can appear to offer, in the words of *Ha'aretz's* former editor-in-chief Hanoch Marmari, "proof of Israel's profound and pervasive evil."

Many of the most extreme *Ha'aretz* writers are also given platforms in the United States, sometimes at fringe outlets but also in mainstream ones.

They're also abundantly cited in such anti-Israel tracts as Stephen Walt and John Mearsheimer's book *The Israel Lobby and U.S. Foreign Policy,* which charges, as you know, that a nefarious collection of groups and people subvert America's best interests in the service of Israel. For instance, chapter three of their book is entitled "A Dwindling Moral Case" and argues Israel is essentially immoral—a conquering, colonizing, racist and militarily brutal nation undeserving of U.S. support. In that chapter's 31 pages there are 53 citations to *Ha'aretz,* many enlisted to underscore the author's charges.

Ha'aretz, by the way, has defended Walt and Mearsheimer editorially and published sympathetic guest commentary on their book.

Here's what Stephen Walt had to say on Bloomberg TV's "Night Talk" with Mike Schneider on October 9, singling out for praise three *Ha'aretz* writers:

> If you look at coverage of, say, Israel policy in Israel itself you'll find many people who are openly very critical and they write every week in publications like *Ha'aretz* and the *Jerusalem Post,* but if you come to the United States you'll never find people like Akiva Eldar, people like Gideon Levy, people like Amira Hass.

Akiva Eldar

Amira Hass

Gideon Levy

These three writers—Akiva Eldar, Gideon Levy and Amira Hass—were famously described by one of Israel's most renowned journalists, Nahum Barnea of *Yediot Ahranot,* in November 2000 as reporters who don't pass the "lynch test." That is, they could not bring themselves to criticize the Palestinian Arabs even when two Israelis were savagely murdered by a Palestinian lynch mob in Ramallah.

Barnea wrote:

> And then the lynch test came, and before it the test of the shooting and fire bombs of the Tanzim fighters, and before it the test of the violations of the Oslo Agreement by Arafat, and it turns out that the support of some reporters [for Palestinian positions] is absolute ... they have a mission.

So. It may have been true years ago that reporters such as these could assail Israel falsely, unfairly, relentlessly and—as Barnea indicates—without mercy even in the nation's darkest hours, but this all happened in Hebrew, causing little outside impact. Not any longer.

It is also clear, as I'll discuss, that the paper simply does not hew to what in America is considered the fundamental responsibility of a serious news operation: factual accuracy and accountability for any errors made.

Many of the errors and extreme distortions purveyed in *Ha'aretz* center on the very themes fueling biased anti-Israel propaganda globally—its alleged racism, discrimination, brutality, immorality and exploitation of Arabs generally.

Danny Rubenstein

Consider the recent example of Danny Rubenstein, *Ha'aretz's* Arab affairs reporter and member of the editorial board.

He was invited by Britain's Zionist Federation to appear on a panel in London celebrating Israel's 60th anniversary. En route and via a flight paid for by the World Zionist Organization, Rubenstein took a detour to Brussels to speak at a UN event sponsored by its Committee on the Exercise of the Inalienable Rights of the Palestinian People. There was no doubt from the outset this would be a virulent, mendacious assault on the Jewish state. And it was.

In the midst of the assemblage demonizing his country and calling for boycotts against it, Rubenstein rose to denounce Israel as an apartheid state. In the firestorm that followed upon his denunciation being publicized—and his speaking engagement for the Zionist Federation cancelled—he declared by way of justification that he would say what he pleases and that his own paper routinely calls Israel apartheid.

He's correct. The paper now uses this—politically and diplomatically the most damning indictment of our era—regularly.

In just the last few weeks, for instance, *Ha'aretz* repeatedly used the term. On October 2, 2007, a column by Amira Hass deplored what she terms "the apartheid laws and orders, military attacks, hidden information, economic siege, land expropriation, expanding settlements and more." She urges Israelis to join in toppling "the apartheid regime we have created here."

It may have been true years ago that reporters such as these could assail Israel falsely, unfairly, relentlessly and—as Nahum Barnea indicates—without mercy even in the nation's darkest hours, but this all happened in Hebrew, causing little outside impact. Not any longer.

And one day later, October 3, an editorial—the voice of the paper—made it formal, stigmatizing Israel as guilty of "political apartheid."

All those Jews and others who have disputed and challenged media outlets from the *New York Times* to Britain's *Guardian* newspaper for publishing the apartheid calumny will find *Ha'aretz* invoked, no doubt, as evidence in support of the claim.

Amos Shocken told me personally, without hesitation, that he considers Israel apartheid in its policies.

Amos Shocken

My conversation a year ago with him was prompted by related allegations in the pages of *Ha'aretz* that were being echoed in America. Amira Hass had repeatedly charged that Israel maintains "Jewish-only" roads in the West Bank, which is completely false. Yet this specific charge is being cited now as evidence of the general apartheid slander. On U.S. campuses, in our newspapers, and on the Internet we find this supposed proof of racist discrimination.

And here is where we see very starkly the corruption—no other word for it—of a newspaper supposedly dispensing factual, reliable information.

It is apparent to anyone driving in the West Bank that there is no religious litmus test for traversing the roads there. Israeli Arabs—Muslim and Christian—move freely and regularly. When I mentioned the *Ha'aretz* claim to an Arab friend, he laughed. He drives routinely on the roads to visit his mother in a West Bank town. In many parts of the West Bank, when there is quiet, Palestinian Arab residents of the territories also use the roads—though there are obviously times and places when they are prevented from doing so for reasons of security.

Need we say these are legitimate security reasons. Innocent Israelis of all faiths—Jewish, Christian and Muslim Israelis—have been murdered on these roads.

Yet Amira Hass, for example, writes: "there's a road for Jews only, like the Modi'in-Givat Ze'ev road..." That is, route 443.

For Jews only?

Here's a gas station owned by the Israeli Arab Hawaja family on that road, route 443.

Here is an Arab woman shopping at the Arab-owned gas station convenience store on Rt. 443.

Here is an Arab shuttle bus passing through. In the foreground is a car with Arab passengers.

Here's another shuttle bus, the kind that passes continuously to and fro carrying both Israeli Arabs and Palestinians with papers allowing entry into Israel.

Here are the Arab passengers in the car above.

All on the Modi'in-Givat Zeev road that Hass says is for Jews only.

Why is all this important? Why do we focus on these particulars? Why do we call for corrections on this from *Ha'aretz?*

Because the charge of apartheid is false—and dangerous. This Jewish-only roads allegation is an example cited as proof, but it's absurd and evaporates when you examine it.

How Amos Shocken answered readers urging correction of the falsehood is revealing.

He writes in one instance:

> I must agree with you; facts mentioned in opinion pieces should be correct. Nevertheless, the term 'roads for Jews only' which may be 'mathematically' incorrect, is fine with me because it describes the true nature and purpose of the roads.

In another note, he writes:

> Your legalistic response is exactly the type that is used to blur reality, rather than clarify it .... It is utterly ridiculous not to call these roads Apartheid roads, because the entire presence of Jews in the occupied territories is of Apartheid nature (not between Whites and Blacks, but between Jewish settlers and Palestinians). (Nov 17, 2005)

So. *Ha'aretz* doesn't just argue, as it's clearly entitled to do in its opinion pages, that it opposes and deplores Jewish settlements or Israel's presence in the West Bank or the difficulties of innocent Palestinian Arabs affected by Israeli military restrictions. The paper willfully and repeatedly prints factually false statements. These defame Israel internationally as racist in the service of forcing the political solution *Ha'aretz* seeks.

Briefly, to remind us what apartheid actually meant: It was wholly and entirely a regime of racial separation and discrimination institutionalised by law in every aspect of daily life, imposed by the white minority and premised on belief in white racial superiority.

Listen to the words of South African-born Benjamin Pogrunda, former editor of the *Rand Daily Mail*. An Israeli now, he shares some of the political views of *Ha'aretz* editorialists—he's a critic of Jewish settlements and of the path of Israel's security barrier. However, Pogrund writes:

> Israel is accused by some of being 'the new apartheid' state. If true, it would be a grave charge, justifying international condemnation and sanctions. But it isn't true. Anyone who knows what apartheid was, and who knows Israel today, is aware of that. Use of the apartheid label is at best ignorant and naive and at worst cynical and manipulative. ...

"**[CAMERA's] legalistic response is exactly the type that is used to blur reality, rather than clarify it .... It is utterly ridiculous not to call these roads Apartheid roads, because the entire presence of Jews in the occupied territories is of Apartheid nature (not between Whites and Blacks, but between Jewish settlers and Palestinians)." (Nov 17, 2005)**

—Amos Schocken

Jonathan Lis (May 17, 2006) claimed that "since 1967, almost no building permits have been issued for the eastern part" of Jerusalem—that is, the heavily Arab side. This is a canard repeated endlessly in propaganda against Israel.

He continues:

> The word 'Bantustan' is often used to describe Israel's policy about a future Palestinian state. It might look like that, superficially. But the root causes— and even more, the intentions—are different. White South Africans invented the Bantustans to pen blacks into defined areas that served as reservoirs of labour; blacks were allowed to leave only when needed to work in white South Africa's factories, farms, offices and homes. The Israeli aim is the exact opposite: it is to keep Palestinians out, having as little to do with them as possible, and letting in as few as possible to work.

> If Israel were to annex the West Bank and control voteless Palestinians as a source of cheap labour—or for religious messianic reasons or strategic reasons —that could indeed be analogous to apartheid. But it is not the intention except in the eyes of a minority—.... who speak of 'transfer' to clear Palestinians out of the West Bank.

There are other serious, repeated factual errors consistent with *Ha'aretz's* general editorial view of Israel as a reprobate nation in need of cudgeling into better behavior.

To mention just a few:

A report by *Ha'aretz* correspondent Jonathan Lis (May 17, 2006) claimed that "since 1967, almost no building permits have been issued for the eastern part" of Jerusalem—that is, the heavily Arab side. This is a canard repeated endlessly in propaganda against Israel as well as in respectable American newspapers. The message is, once more, that Israel is ruthlessly denying Arabs the very basic needs of providing their families with housing.

In fact, according to multiple in-depth studies, thousands of building permits

Based on a graph by Justus Reid Weiner of the Jerusalem Center for Public Affairs, about ?00 permits were issued ?etween 1967 and 2001.

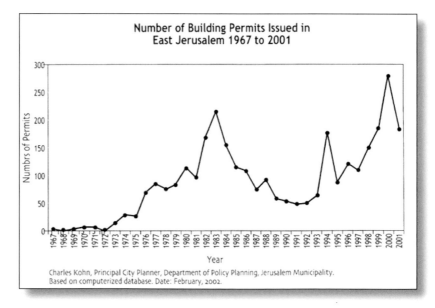

Number of Building Permits Issued in East Jerusalem 1967 to 2001

Charles Kohn, Principal City Planner, Department of Policy Planning, Jerusalem Municipality. Based on computerized database. Date: February, 2002.

have been issued and many thousands more are available. Based on a graph by Justus Reid Weiner of the Jerusalem Center for Public Affairs, about 3000 permits were issued between 1967 and 2001.

As Weiner's study notes, "the percentage of applications that result in the issuance of a building permit is virtually identical in Arab and Jewish neighborhoods" of Jerusalem. Furthermore, the study shows, the city has "authorize[d] the issuance of in excess of 36,000 permits for new housing units in the Arab sector," suggesting that the number of permits issued to the Arab sector could be much higher if only more individuals from that sector would apply for permits.

We're speaking here only of legal building, of course. Illegal Arab building in and around Jerusalem is widespread, the structures often luxurious. The phenomenon goes essentially unchecked by the occasional house demolition—frequently misleading news media reports notwithstanding. According to Weiner, "Illegal construction has reached epidemic proportions. A senior Palestinian official boasted that they have built 6,000 homes without permits during the last 4 years, of which less than 200 were demolished by the city."

Where *Ha'aretz* could and should be reporting essential information, it is instead furthering erroneous claims of discriminatory treatment of Arabs.

One last example of the material falsehoods that appear in *Ha'aretz* was a piece by Itzhak Laor. To give you an idea of the tenor of his views, he participated in a 2006 event in Dublin, Ireland with the Ireland Palestine Solidarity Campaign at which he denounced Israeli policies and was quoted in *The Irish Times* saying: "I'm ashamed of my country, of my government and of the violence of the Israeli state." In *Ha'aretz* he charged:

> Most [Israeli] Arabs were forced to become day laborers. No industry was ever established in their villages. Industry in Israel—whether in the private or public sector—was always built with state assistance.

> But the most important issue involves the numbers that cannot be disputed: Today 1,340,200 people live on those very lands that were granted to them when they totaled 160,000 and were pushed off their lands.

Again, what of the facts?

The charge that "most" of the land owned by Israeli Arabs was "expropriated" is fiction. The land belonging to Arabs who fled in 1948 was expropriated, but those who remained in Israel retained theirs. Arabs—though they're just 20% of the population—own about half the private land and have equal access to the roughly 80% of Israel that is government-owned state land. In practice and under new court rulings they also have access to JNF land.

Similarly, in charging that Arabs were forced to become "day laborers," Laor

Where *Ha'aretz* could and should be reporting relevant facts, it is instead furthering erroneous claims of discriminatory treatment of Arabs.

characterizes a trend toward urbanization—occurring across the globe—as a particular affliction wrought by cruel Jewish Israelis upon Arabs. In America 2.5 percent of the labor force are farmers, a figure comparable to Jews in Israel, while among Israeli Arabs 5 percent are in farming.

Equally ludicrous is Laor's charge that "no industry was ever established in their villages" and that industry has always developed with government assistance. In reality, industrial parks are commonplace in Israeli Arab towns, including Baqa al-Garbiya, Um al-Fahm, Sakhnin, Yirka, Nazareth, Acco and myriad other communities. Imad Younis, founder of Alpha Omega, a successful Nazareth biotech company, Tamim Yassin of Obek Gaz and Ali Kadmani of Kadmani Metal Works are among successful Israeli Arab businessmen invisible to the columnist. Much development is private but government assistance also plays a part, as in such enterprises as "industrial estates."

A December 2005 *Jerusalem Post* article reports "the Arab sector experienced a surge in entrepreneurial activity in recent years" and notes that some 7 percent of Intel's hi-tech workers in the country—or 500 engineers—are Arab. According to employee Nabil Sakhran: "Many of the Arab engineers are among the technological leaders in the company, and are in senior managerial positions."

Laor's error-ridden caricatures of Israel can only fuel prejudice and enmity toward the country.

With virtually every crisis, various *Ha'aretz* commentators level attacks on Israel that swiftly enter the wider information world. Despite, for instance, numerous *Ha'aretz* editorialists, staff writers and guest contributors strongly endorsing Israel's moral right and obligation to respond decisively to the kidnapping of a soldier near Gaza and to Hezbollah's attacks in the summer of 2006, many other writers and contributors severely castigated the government on ethical grounds—and those attacks were picked up and echoed across the globe. Indeed, the more extreme and hysterical the commentary, the more avidly quoted beyond Israel's shores.

Consider the ripple effect of such writing, including that of Gideon Levy. From the beginning of July 2006 when the conflict with Hamas intensified, he repeatedly wrote in harsh denunciation of Israel. With the barest of reference to Israeli rights and vulnerabilities or to the irredentism of its adversary, he charged on July 2 that the government's efforts to rescue kidnapped Gilad Shalit and to halt the rain of rockets inside Israel from Gaza make Israel indistinguishable "from a terror organization."

Levy penned a piece on July 16—four days after the rain of Hezbollah katyushas began, driving hundreds of thousands of Israelis into shelters, killing and maiming innocents and setting forests and fields on fire. He assailed Israel as the neighborhood's "loudmouth bully," mocking the nation's response to the kidnapping of soldiers and charging that Israel likes war. According to Levy, "we're eager to get to the battlefield and the killing without delay, without taking any time to think. That deepens suspicions that we need a war every few years ..."

On August 6, Levy led his column with: "This miserable war in Lebanon, which is just getting more and more complicated for no reason at all, was born in Israel's greed for land."

On August 13, believing Israel had fared badly in the war, he applauded the outcome as a positive development, one that might teach the war-like state a lesson, including changing "our ways and our language, the language we speak to our neighbors with violence and force."

Not only did scores of Web sites hostile to Israel—including the Holocaust-revisionist Institute for Historical Review—post many of Levy's columns, but newspapers from Australia to Ireland to Canada, America and Japan cited various of his charges.

Yet at the same time, in anguished essays written as Israel endured the unchecked rocket barrages of the Hezbollah war, *Ha'aretz* columnist Ari Shavit excoriated Israeli elites, including those in the news media. Theirs was a debilitating assault on Israeli society, with "their unending attacks, both direct and indirect ... on the Zionist narrative ..." He called urgently for "clarification and clarity" to restore the nation's spirit and resolve. Though he spoke generally of the enervating effects on society of such attacks, he might have added—were it possible—that his own newspaper has been a primary engine of Israel's denigration—internally and internationally.

All who understand that the information battleground is global need to challenge the paper's violation of basic journalistic ethics. *Ha'aretz's* biased and false reporting affects all of us.

Panel Discussion
Jewish Defamation of Israel: Roots, Rationales, and Ramifications

by Edward Alexander, moderator*

Our subject is "Israel's Jewish Defamers." Let me begin with a 1988 quotation from the Israeli novelist, Aharon Appelfeld:

> Antisemitism directed at oneself was an original Jewish creation. I don't know of any other nation so flooded with self-criticism. Even after the Holocaust ... harsh comments were made by prominent Jews against the victims ...The Jewish ability to internalize any critical and condemnatory remark and castigate themselves is one of the marvels of human nature .... Day and night ... that feeling produces dread, sensitivity, self-criticism and sometimes self-destruction.

The Jewish dimension of this subject has a very long history. In Isaiah 49: 17 we read: "Thy destroyers and they that make thee waste shall come forth from thee."

Most of the numerous recent books about the antisemitism of Israel-hatred allude to the "new" antisemitism, or (in French) "les nouvelles vagues de l'antisemitisme." Yet the Jewish dimension of this subject has a very long history. In Isaiah 49: 17 we read: ["m'harsayich u-meicharivayich mimeich yeitz'u]/ Thy destroyers and they that make thee waste shall come forth from thee". Before Pope Gregory IX ordered the Talmud to be seized, examined, and publicly burnt in Paris and Rome, he was presented in 1239 with a detailed analysis of

---

Edward Alexander is professor emeritus of English at the University of Washington in Seattle. He is the author of numerous books, including The Jewish Wars: Reflections by One of the Belligerents; Irving Howe — Socialist, Critic, Jew; The Holocaust and the War of Ideas; *and, most recently,* The Jewish Divide Over Israel: Accusers and Defenders, *co-authored with Paul Bogdanor.*

the evils of Jewish religious books by Nicholas Donin, a Jewish convert to Catholicism. In the 16th century, Martin Luther's seemingly innovative program of burning synagogues, destroying Jewish homes, confiscating the Talmud and all other Jewish religious books, was in fact derived from the proposals of Johannes (formerly Josef) Pfefferkorn, the Jewish convert who had years earlier exhorted his German countrymen to "drive the old Jews out like dirty dogs and baptize their young children."

Brazenly leaping ahead several centuries, let us listen to Irving Howe writing in 1970 about the New Left:

> Jewish boys and girls, children of the generation that saw Auschwitz, hate democratic Israel and celebrate as 'revolutionary' the Egyptian dictatorship. Some of them pretend to be indifferent to the anti-Jewish insinuations of the Black Panthers; a few go so far as to collect money for Al-Fatah, which pledges to take Tel-Aviv. About this, I cannot say more; it is simply too painful.

One understands what Howe meant. The hatred for Israel among the Jewish divisions of the New Left was already intense, even if it had not yet reached the point where it is today, when such Jews believe or at least allege that Israel, from their humanitarian and progressive perspective, is evil incarnate, to a degree that transcends the wickedness of any other state that exists or ever existed. To allege this, or to couple the Star of David with the Nazi swastika is NOT just to express criticism of the policies of one or another Israeli government (as people like the aforementioned Howe often did); it is to defame Israel by association with the most powerful symbol of evil, of that which must be uprooted from the face of the earth.

A critic, as John Stuart Mill once wrote, need not be an enemy; but the people of whom we speak today are not critics of the Jewish state, but its sworn enemies. Matthew Arnold, in a classic statement of 1865, said that "the function of criticism is to see the object as in itself it really is." He did not say that the function of criticism is to erase or obliterate or destroy the object.

The disproportionate influence of Jewish defamers of Israel depends on the fact that most of them demonize Israel precisely as Jews; indeed, it is often their demonization of Israel that makes them Jews. For them the old wisecrack (in a Haim Hazaz story of 1942) that "when a man can no longer be a Jew, he becomes a Zionist" no longer applies. They embody a new reality:

> When a man can no longer be a Jew, he becomes an anti-Zionist. By declaring themselves in favor of Jewish powerlessness they announce—in a kind of moral get-rich-quick scheme, a grasp at virtue without responsibility—both their purity and their Jewishness.

If we turn our eyes from the antics of Israel's Jewish defamers to the object of their defamation, the people and the land of Israel and their constant burden of peril, we may well be tempted to repeat Mark Anthony's words as he addresses

Matthew Arnold, in a classic statement of 1865, said that "the function of criticism is to see the object as in itself it really is." He did not say that the function of criticism is to erase or obliterate or destroy the object.

The disproportionate influence of Jewish defamers of Israel depends on the fact that most of them demonize Israel precisely as Jews; indeed, it is often their demonization of Israel that makes them Jews.

the ravaged body of Julius Caesar: "Pardon me, [thou bleeding piece of earth,] that I am meek and gentle with these butchers."

THE PANELISTS

All of us qualify as experts according to the Mark Twain definition: "an expert is a guy from out of town": Alvin Rosenfeld from Indiana, Kenneth Levin from Boston, Cynthia Ozick from New Rochelle, myself from Seattle.

CYNTHIA OZICK

Our first speaker is Cynthia Ozick. She is the author of more than a dozen award-winning works of fiction and essays. Her essay collection *Quarrel and Quandry* won the 2001 National Book Critic Circle Award, and *Fame and Folly* was a finalist for the 1996 Pulitzer Prize. She is widely recognized, to quote the English critic John Sutherland, as "the most accomplished and graceful literary stylist of our time." Her topic today is: "Reflections on Apostasy."

ALVIN ROSENFELD

Our second speaker is Alvin Rosenfeld, professor of English and Jewish Studies at Indiana University, author of many books on Jewish subjects, and of the now world-famous monograph called "Progressive Jewish Thought and the New Antisemitism." When I watch, as I sometimes do, the Discovery Channel's "Dirty Jobs" program, which features people who, for the general welfare, work amidst filth of every variety, I often expect to see Alvin, wearing the mental equivalent of hip-boots, wading through the mire of Israel-hatred generated by the Progressive Jews about whom he has written. His topic today is "What is 'Criticism of Israel'"?

KENNETH LEVIN

Kenneth Levin holds degrees in mathematics, English, medicine, and history. He is a clinical instructor in psychiatry at Harvard University and maintains a private practice in psychiatry. The best-known of his books is *The Oslo Syndrome: Delusions of a People Under Siege.* It is both a political history of Israel and a study of the relationship of Jews to the Jewish state of Israel. Cynthia Ozick has called it "the most important manifesto of our generaion, an indispensable analysis that explains the present and may yet save the future."

Apostasy, Then and Now

by Cynthia Ozick

Apostasy among Jews has a long tradition. In its most literal expression under the hegemony of the medieval Church, apostasy meant conversion to Christianity—and something more. The apostate felt obliged to confirm, and to prove, his new commitment by initiating even harsher persecutions than those already customary. And, of course, the apostate was in one respect far better credentialed and equipped for perfidious Jewish inventions than his Christian compatriots. Even as a former Jew, even having repudiated his old identity, it was explicitly as a Jew that he was called upon to be useful, since it was by virtue of his being a Jew that he could be regarded as authoritative, and his views as authentic.

As an authentic and authoritative Jew, clearly he was privy to the inmost heart of Jewish arcana, and uniquely positioned to expose it for what it was, for the wickedness and blasphemy it harbored. Franciscans and Dominicans might intuit that the Talmud was the source of enmity to Christianity and mockery of the Saviour, but with no access to its literature, they were helpless to produce the evidence. With Jewish apostasy zealously in its service, all clerical doubt vanished. The miscreant Jews could be authentically and authoritatively punished, according to the principle of divine supersessionism, by all the merciless means at the disposal of Christian piety.

The apostate prevaricated; the clerisy believed. Who benefited from this collusion? The holy friars certainly, since their religious convictions, requiring the suffering of Jews in recompense for the Crucifixion, were further stimulated and fed; and also the local monarchs: influenced by the friars, they regularly profited from pressure on the Jews, whether through impoverishing taxation or, more directly, through confiscation and pillage.

And for ordinary folk witnessing a mammoth bonfire of Torah scrolls and volumes of Talmud sending their flames into the sky, where the angels dwell, there was the holiday elation and uplift of soul a communal festivity always ignites.

But what of the apostates themselves? How did such impressive figures as Nicholas Donin and Pablo Christiani fare? From being despised as societal pariahs they were instantly elevated to honored public pundits. They were intelligent men —they were, in fact, sophisticated intellectuals. Were they cynical political opportunists with an instinct for where the power lies? Were they thoughtful pragmatists who for the sake of quotidian ease simply determined that it is prudent to belong to the safe majority rather than to a harassed minority?

Or were they genuine believers who had been persuaded of the higher truth of Christianity? An apostate in those times may have been any of these—but whatever his motivation, the apostate had to recognize, in full awareness, that he was

> **The apostate felt obliged to confirm, and to prove, his new commitment by initiating even harsher persecutions than those already customary. And, of course, the apostate was in one respect far better credentialed and equipped for perfidious Jewish inventions than his Christian compatriots.**

entering into a virulent bargain: the price for his acceptance, and his ascent, was to increase the anguish of the Jews he was leaving behind.

As with the apostasy of individuals, so with the mega-apostasies of world history. When developing Christianity, whatever its motivations and convictions, departed from Judaism, it was the Jews who were made to suffer. When developing Islam, whatever its motivations and convictions, departed from Judaism and Christianity, it was again the Jews who were made to suffer. Christianity belatedly reformed itself, latterly through shame in the face of the Holocaust, initially through loss of the temporal power to enforce the old theologically instigated crimes. Islam, its Islamist branches notoriously supported and succored by states, awaits its own reformation.

But perhaps these huge collective movements, evolving through the centuries with all their internal divisions and kaleidoscopic complexities, can no longer be defined as apostasies. Christianity, while not forsaking its central messianic creed, has come to regard itself, in the words of Pope John XXIII, as Judaism's younger brother. Islam, by contrast, far from seeing itself as derivative or fraternal, points to both Judaism and Christianity as apostasies willfully broken away from the original—hence the purest—source of God's word, the Koran.

How, then, should we look at this word apostate today? ... The apostate is one who defames—if not his origins explicitly, then his living counterparts, the people to whom he was born.

How, then, should we look at this word apostate today? That it has mostly fallen into disuse we know; yet its freight has been put to many uses, especially under the noose of successive creedal tyrannies. Inevitably, in contemporary terms, it returns us to the theme of defamation. The apostate is one who defames—if not his origins explicitly, then his living counterparts, the people to whom he was born.

In the Soviet Union, for instance, the Yevsektsia, the "Jew section" of the Communist Party, composed of avowed Communists "of Jewish descent," was an instrument of the oppression of Jews. As for the present moment, though the medieval Church is no more than a literary memory in the mind of the largely secular West, and the Soviet Union is gone, the notion of apostasy, as applied to the individual, still holds. But its meaning has been curiously reversed. The Nicholas Donins and Pablo Christianis of ages past ran to abandon their Jewish ties even as they subverted them. The Nicholas Donins and Pablo Christianis of our own time run to embrace their Jewish ties even as they besmirch them.

So it is as self-declared Jews, as loyal and honorable Jews, as Jews in the line of the prophets, as Jews who speak out for the sake of the integrity of Jews and Judaism, that we nowadays hear arguments against the survival, or the necessity, or the legitimacy, of the State of Israel. These negating Jewish voices can be lyrical, as from the poets; or nimble, as from the novelists; or transcendent, as from the philosophers; or dour, as from the revisionist historians; or pragmatic, as from the realists; or apoplectically apocalyptical, as from the unregenerate Marxists; or Houdinishly knotted, as from the theologians; or self-referential, as from all of the above. They include, among innumerable well-known others,

So it is as self-declared Jews, as loyal and honorable Jews, as Jews in the line of the prophets, as Jews who speak out for the sake of the integrity of Jews and Judaism, that we nowadays hear arguments against the survival, or the necessity, or the legitimacy, of the State of Israel.

Adrienne Rich and Irena Klepfisz and Jacqueline Rose and Judith Butler and George Steiner and Tony Judt and Marc Ellis—and, most engagingly, Michael Lerner.

I am compelled to call Lerner engaging, even entertaining, because there is something of the mime about him—a very garrulous mime. Yet he can, like the late Marcel Marceau, assume a particular pose with lifelike effect, and then instantly go on to contort into a wondrously different persona. His latest role is that of rabbi. Despite his history as a dropout from the Jewish Theological Seminary's rabbinical school, Rabbi Lerner, as we must now call him, was belatedly eased into the rabbinate through a "private ordination" at the hands of Rabbi Zalman Schachter-Shalomi, holder of the Chair in World Wisdom at the Naropa Institute in Colorado, the Buddhist center beloved by Allen Ginsberg, and if you should wish to cast doubt on Lerner's rabbinic validity or the competence of his rabbinic learning, you may see the proof of it in the little white knitted yarmulke he sports while discoursing with Bill Moyers on television, speaking in one breath both of the perniciousness of the "Israel lobby" and of the urgency of universal love.

In addition to his prestigious clerical status, Rabbi Lerner is renowned as the founder and editor of *Tikkun,* a magazine specifically designed to counter the influence of *Commentary*. *Tikkun's* political affinities lie with the *Nation,* though in the writing of English it is radically inferior to almost every other journal intended for grownups, especially when it is Rabbi Lerner who is doing the writing. As a journalist, as a polemicist, as a putative philosopher, Rabbi Lerner is chaotic, disorganized, frequently ungrammatical, self-contradictory, puerile, and unbearably long-winded.

If you should wish to cast doubt on Michael Lerner's rabbinic validity or the competence of his rabbinic learning, you may see the proof of it in the little white knitted yarmulke he sports while discoursing with Bill Moyers on television, speaking in one breath both of the perniciousness of the "Israel lobby" and of the urgency of universal love.

Nevertheless, his central point always comes through with radiant repetitive clarity: Israel is culpable, Israel is wicked, Israel is an oppressor, and so on. By now nearly everyone understands that tikkun means "repair of the world"; it is one of those many noble terms, like "peace," "justice," and "human rights," that have been despoiled and betrayed by Orwellian political chicanery.

Michael Lerner

To create a new magazine—even if inspired by envy and spite—is impressive enough. But Rabbi Lerner is also the founder of at least two aspiring social movements. Decades ago, when—still in the bloom of youth and declaring that "the synagogue as currently established will have to be smashed"—he headed the Seattle Liberation Front, an enterprise as pugnacious as its name. After a dustup with the police, he was arrested and tried as one of the honored Seattle Seven. According to Rabbi Lerner, the violence was not of the Front's making, and his sentence of several months in jail was unjustly imposed. But the world has since moved on; except for creaky old Cuba and vim-and-virulence Venezuela, Liberation Fronts are no longer in fashion, having been replaced by the softer urgencies of Spirituality.

By now the time had surely come for the founding of a front more in conformity with the present—hence Rabbi Lerner's most recent coinage: the NSP, the Network of Spiritual Progressives. Never mind the treacly oxymoronic rubric. It is a curiosity in itself that "progressive" has lately been resuscitated in common parlance. An amnesiac generation has forgotten that this term, as embraced by Stalin's Western cadres, was once so steeped in earned opprobrium and shame that it seemed likely to vanish forever, along with that other lost political ideal, Kinder, Kuche, Kirche.

"Progressive," however, has turned out to be a boomerang: it goes away only to return, its threadbare mantras intact. Those old progressives, aka fellow travelers, were, like Stalin himself, hard-headed, hard-hearted atheists: not for them this gossamer, vapid winged thing, composed of vaporous rainbows and spun sugar, called Spirituality.

With consummate ingenuity, Rabbi Lerner's Network of Spiritual Progressives manages to link scurrility with sentimental religiosity: only imagine Karl Marx davening, and you will comprehend the dazzlement of Rabbi Lerner's current achievement. Lately, as it happens, he has added yet another element to his mix: perhaps the NSP will soon morph into the NSPR, the Network of Spiritual Progressive Realists. Should this come to pass, it will be because Rabbi Lerner, mentor to many, has acquired two celebrated mentors of his own: John J. Mearsheimer and Stephen M. Walt, academics noted for political realism, and co-authors of the problematic *The Israel Lobby and U. S. Foreign Policy*.

In an article typically prolix and moistly dedicated to the common good, Rabbi Lerner, with some minuscule demurrals, strides in lockstep with these eminent representatives of the realist school. Not only does he parallel and support their conclusions, but he is able to go beyond their limited analysis. After all, as a faithful Jew, and certainly as a rabbi, he is in possession of a privileged intimacy with internal American Jewish society, which the two professors naturally lack, and can only surmise and invent. Besides, Mearsheimer and Walt, in their scrupulous civility, while condemning what they take to be large public conspiracies, are careful not to intrude on the individual practices of synagogues and households.

Rabbi Lerner, mentor to many, has acquired two celebrated mentors of his own: John J. Mearsheimer and Stephen M. Walt, academics noted for political realism, and co-authors of the problematic *The Israel Lobby and U. S. Foreign Policy*.

Not so Rabbi Lerner. "First," he writes, "the Israel lobby cannot be understood apart from the vast number of Jewish institutions and even individual communities, synagogues, and families that impose on their members a certain discipline that goes well beyond any normal political party or force, challenging the human, ethical, and Jewish identities of anyone who disagrees with its fundamental assumptions."

Let us interrupt for a moment to reprise one brief passage: a certain discipline that goes well beyond any normal political party or force. Of what notorious nineteenth-century czarist fabrication, the favorite of neo-Nazis and their admirers, do these words remind us? Who and where are those sinister Jewish families, including teens and toddlers, whose lives are devoted to the machinations of this amorphous lobby? As for the synagogues, when a shul is discovered openly raising funds to purchase an ambulance for an Israeli town daily attacked by rockets, is that shul an active branch of the Israel lobby? And what precisely is the nature of this "discipline," and on whom is it exerted? I will readily testify that I was not knowingly under the imposition of a discipline, or compelled by any party or mysterious force, when of my own free will I once had the pleasure, in public, of dubbing the pre-rabbinic Lerner an "intellectual wimp." Is it possible that this rude ad hominem, and several other rudenesses herein, will qualify me as a member in good standing of the Israel lobby?

It is easy to dismiss, even to lampoon, Michael Lerner. His magazine is negligible; his Network of Spiritual Progressives is risible. But he is one of a growing band of vocal and ambitious self-touting Jews whose hostility to the State of Israel more and more takes on the character of the spite that kills. The noise they make they call a silencing. The debate they attract they call a censoring.

The answer is plainly yes, and Rabbi Lerner has already fingered me in print. "I am sure," he goes on, "that the instinctive reaction of a large section of the American Jewish community affiliated with the Jewish lobby will be the predictable assault on Mearsheimer and Walt and on *Tikkun* and on anyone else who speaks up in criticism of the Israel lobby." And having praised "the often careful and thoughtful work of Mearsheimer and Walt," while also conceding that he has been "referring frequently with their permission" to their book, he offers this comment: "The Israel lobby has become a major perpetrator of the fear orientation in politics that the NSP believes to be at the heart of the many problems facing the world. The Israel lobby sees threats everywhere."

Rabbi Lerner and his reality instructors perhaps do not see threats? Of course they do -- the multiple threats that flow from American policies toward Israel, controlled and manipulated by the Israel lobby; and it is the Israel lobby that stands in the way of world peace and serenity by inciting the enmity of Ahmadinejad and all other jihadists determined to annihilate the Jewish state. Rabbi Lerner emphasizes in a headline: "AIPAC Has Democratic Congresspeople Scared." In fact, so scared of the Israel lobby are Democrats and Republicans alike, that—as Rabbi Lerner writes elsewhere—he "would not be surprised to learn that some branch of our government conspired either actively to promote or passively to allow" the agony of the Towers. Ah, and who scares and influences and virtually runs the government? The Israel lobby. Here Rabbi Lerner joins unclean hands with Amiri Baraka and Rosie O'Donnell.

As a scholar (he claims two doctorates), Rabbi Lerner has not troubled so much as to glance at the masses of serious analytic criticism exposing his mentors' unprofessional methods, reliance on secondary and tertiary journalism, errors of fact, errors of recent history, and promulgation of shameless ancient charges; instead, he repeats their vilifications and lauds their "careful and thoughtful work."

It is easy to dismiss, even to lampoon, Michael Lerner. His magazine is negligible; his Network of Spiritual Progressives is risible. But he is one of a growing band of vocal and ambitious self-touting Jews whose hostility to the State of Israel more and more takes on the character of the spite that kills. The noise they make they call a silencing. The debate they attract they call a censoring. Some despise nationalism and the nation-state on principle, while at the same time arguing for Palestinian national rights.

The insouciant Tony Judt flicks off Israel as an "anachronism." Jacqueline Rose, feverishly psychoanalytical, weaves eros into murder, seeing in suicide bombing an "unbearable intimacy . . . an act of passionate identification . . . a deadly embrace." Adrienne Rich asks Zionism, the term and its history, "to dissolve before twenty-first century realities": the malevolent siege of Israel, to be sure, is not such a reality. Judith Butler desires her status as a Jew not to be embarrassed by confusing it with the Zionist project, the disappearance of which she longs to accomplish. And in a didactic work of fiction, the lofty George Steiner taints the establishment of Israel with the ultimate taint: he credits Hitler with the invention of Zionism, and Judaism with the invention of Hitler.

Nicholas Donin and Pablo Christiani, those clever old friars much experienced in crushing Jewish cultural and political expression, would feel right at home in this company, as clever as themselves: they would sympathize with the familiar sensibility of Jews eager to join the dominating class in a period when the dominating class is hurtful to Jews. But how puzzled they might be by this new-fangled modern apostasy, whereby the apostates declare how profoundly Jewish they are! And what they might make of the sight of Rabbi Michael Lerner in his yarmulke as he recites the recognizable medieval canards of Mearsheimer and Walt, only God in his heaven can tell.

What is "Criticism of Israel?"

by Alvin Rosenfeld

In a free society, ongoing, open debate of political issues is not only desirable but essential. Pointed, well-informed criticism is the hallmark of such debate. But as Andrea Levin, Alex Safian, and Cynthia Ozick make clear, what Israel and its supporters increasingly confront today is often not, in fact, well-informed criticism but a robust and growing hostility that typically expresses itself through hateful and almost always falsifying words and calls itself, misleadingly, "criticism of Israel."

Like all democracies, Israel benefits from smart, tough-minded criticism and draws no end of it from commentators within its borders as well as from without. But much of what passes these days as "criticism of Israel" is full of ill-will and so obviously intent on spreading slanted information and even misinformation as to constitute something else, something akin to a new and malign literary and political genre. It has its own inner logic, its own conventions, its own narrative thrust, and its own predictable outcome. One of these conventions, as we shall soon see, is that the person using this new genre is often him or herself a Jew. By publicly proclaiming that he or she is indeed a Jew, the practitioner of "criticism of Israel" looks to bestow hechsher on the toxicity that then flows from the pen and, at the same time, seeks to ward off any suggestion that he or she may be guilty of harboring any ingrained hostility toward the Jewish state.

And yet such hostility exists today in abundance, including among some Jews. The specific case will be discussed a bit later. As evidence of a broader and more generalized antipathy to Jews and, especially, the Jewish state, I cite some words that come to us from Denis MacShane. Mr. MacShane does not, in fact, participate in this new genre but opposes it strongly. As his last name indicates, he doesn't have to step before an audience and say that he's Jewish. He's not. Nor were any of the other British parliamentarians that joined him some months ago when, at the behest of Tony Blair, then still prime minister, he had an opportunity to investigate resurgent antisemitism in the United Kingdom.

Denis MacShane

Most of you in this room today are well-read and well-traveled people. No doubt you go back and forth to Europe, and when you're in Europe you probably don't detect any resurgent hostility to Jews. But Mr. MacShane and his colleagues had no trouble, unfortunately, spotting lots of it. In an Op-Ed column ("The New Antisemitism") that he published in *The Washington Post,* September 4, 2007, he writes:

"Hatred of Jews has reached new heights in Europe and many points south and east of the old continent." He then talks about the nature of the report that he handed Prime Minister Blair and says: "Our report showed ... Synagogues attacked. Jewish schoolboys jostled on public transportation. Rabbis punched and knifed. British Jews feeling compelled to raise millions to provide private security for their weddings and community events. On campuses, militant anti-Jewish students fueled by Islamist or far-left hate seeking to prevent Jewish students from expressing their opinions."

It's a worrisome list of ugly, menacing incidents, most of which are not prominently reported in this country and, consequently, are generally unknown here. I'll continue with just two more sentences. "More worrisome," Mr. MacShane adds, "More worrisome was what we described as anti-Jewish discourse, a mood and tone whenever Jews are discussed, whether in the media, at universities, among the liberal media elite or at dinner parties of modish London. To express any support for Israel or any feeling for the right of a Jewish state to exist produces denunciation, even contempt."

This succinct but authoritative inventory of anti-Jewish hostility may come as a surprise, for most of you who travel in Europe are unlikely to feel it. But any synagogue that you pass almost certainly will be guarded, as will be most Jewish schools and other institutions that are identifiably Jewish. And, sad to say, this security is in place out of necessity. The churches usually are not guarded; most of the mosques are not guarded. And for good reason: Constant threats are not typically made against people who go to the churches and the mosques of Europe to pray. But the synagogues do require this kind of protection. Since they require it, it's good that they have it. But the fact that they need it is a scandal, although it's a scandal that goes largely unnoticed.

Six decades and more after the Holocaust, hostility to Jews, Judaism, and the Jewish state should be out of the question in Europe or anywhere else in the world. And yet, as Mr. MacShane's report and countless other studies demonstrate, such hostility has become part of common parlance, sometimes rising to the level of openly-expressed aggression. And the aggression is not always confined to mere rhetoric. There is, in other words, a connection between anti-Semitic acts and anti-Semitic utterances. The words really are important in themselves, and they also give license to aggressive behavior. And so, along with the ugly words are ugly deeds in the form of street-level hostility against Jews and Jewish institutions within Europe and, in the Middle East, against the Jewish state itself.

I note some of the connections between anti-Semitic acts and anti-Semitic utterances in my article, "Progressive Jewish Thought and the New anti-Semitism," which Edward Alexander just referred to. It was published by the American

Jewish Committee and provoked a heated debate about the role of some Jewish "critics of Israel" who call themselves "progressive" but at times express views that align them with those who are aggressively engaged in an on-going intellectual assault against Israel and, sometimes, more broadly against the Jews. A few examples will serve to illustrate.

In June, 2007, Hamas pulled off a violent and successful military coup against Fatah forces in the Gaza Strip. In the course of this fighting, Palestinians killed scores of other Palestinians, sometimes by throwing them alive off of 12- and 15-story buildings or by entering hospitals and murdering the wounded in their beds. Some Fatah members were seized in their homes, dragged out to the streets and murdered in front of their wives and children. There were reports of prisoners having their knee-caps shot off and nails being driven into their legs and other sadistic acts of bodily mutilation. These atrocities were widely reported. However, they provoked relatively little public outcry by human rights groups. Amazingly, some commentators fixed responsibility for these outrageous crimes on Israel and the United States.

For instance, in the midst of this horror in Gaza, Professor Richard Falk, formerly a professor of International Law at Princeton University and more recently a Distinguished Visiting Professor at University of California at Santa Barbara, wrote a widely circulated article called "Slouching Towards a Palestinian Holocaust." Prof. Falk claimed that the situation was morally far worse than the atrocities committed in Rwanda and Srebrenica, Bosnia. To emphasize this point, Prof. Falk evoked the Nazi Holocaust. The following are his words: "It is especially painful for me, as an American Jew, to feel compelled to portray the on-going and intensifying abuse of the Palestinian people by Israel through a reliance on such an inflammatory metaphor as 'holocaust'."

Now, as you know, Israel had vacated the Gaza Strip in August of 2005. Nevertheless, Prof. Falk insists that "the pattern of criminality associated with Israeli policies in Gaza was responsible for producing this latest violence." Yet this was Palestinian-on-Palestinian bloodshed with nary an Israeli soldier to be seen. Prof. Falk, however, goes on to identify a pattern of Israeli complicity that, he claims, was "deliberate" and "geno-

cidal." These words carry a heavy charge. They should remind the world, he argues, of other words, ones we all know well. And to drive home his rhetorical point, he quotes them more than once: "Never again."

Professor Richard Falk

Thinking back, we recall that Gaza during this period was indeed a bloody mess. But wasn't attributing this mess to the Israelis, and comparing it to the Nazi Holocaust, a bit far-fetched? Dr. Falk poses the following question: "Is it an irresponsible overstatement to associate the treatment of the Palestinians with this criminalized Nazi record of collective atrocity?" Most of us would answer unhesitatingly, "Yes, it is indeed irresponsible and shouldn't be said." Falk disagrees. His answer is: "I think not." He offers no evidence whatsoever to support his claim that Israeli treatment of the Palestinians finds an apt historical parallel in the Nazi treatment of the Jews. He offers no such evidence because it simply doesn't exist. Moreover, the Israelis had cleared out of Gaza long before the Palestinian-on-Palestinian bloodletting had begun and had nothing to do with it. Nevertheless, Prof. Falk continues, claiming that "the recent developments in Gaza are especially disturbing because they express so vividly, a deliberate intention on the part of Israel and its allies, to expose an entire human community to life-endangering conditions of utmost cruelty."

Prof. Falk insists, and these again are his words, "the pattern of criminality associated with Israeli policies in Gaza was responsible for producing this latest violence."

Certainly there was cruelty. But Israel in fact had nothing whatsoever to do with tossing Palestinians off the roof-tops of high-rise buildings in Gaza. Other Palestinians were doing that. In Prof. Falk's account, however, an Israeli hand continues somehow-he never tells us how-to direct the murderous actions from afar, shaping it into what he calls "a holocaust in the making."

In the past, to make such a charge was tantamount to committing an act of blood-libel against the Jews. Today, if you are of a certain political persuasion, to make such a charge is considered a legitimate way of speaking out for peace and justice.

Princeton University, where Richard Falk taught for many years, is justifiably regarded to be one of America's outstanding universities. It has one of this country's most eminent academic presses. Yet, as one more illustration of the degree to which irresponsible views on Zionism and Israel have migrated from the margins to the mainstream, Jacqueline Rose's seriously flawed and willfully malicious book, *The Question of Zion,* was published under the Princeton University Press imprint. Among other things, what you'll find if you take a look at this work are the following egregious errors, which I analyze at greater length in "Progressive Jewish Thought and the New Antisemitism":

Jacqueline Rose

According to Jacqueline Rose, Adolph Hitler and Theodore Herzl once attended the Paris Opera House for the same performance of an opera written by Wagner. She doesn't bother to tell us, but I'll simply remind you of what you already know: Herzl died in 1904 and Hitler never stepped foot in Paris before 1940. Thus, there is no way that Hitler and Herzl could have simultaneously attended a Wagner opera in the Paris Opera House. They never met. But they do meet in the pages of her book. What are they doing together there? By bringing them into alignment artificially, Rose is mingling Zionism and Nazism. If you can link the father of Zionism with the father of Nazism, you've pulled off quite something, something that takes us well beyond criticism of Israel into this still-to-be-named genre of hostility which calls itself "criticism of Israel."

You'll also find in Jacqueline Rose's book the claim that the Israel Defense Forces razed the town of Jenin following the bombing at Pesach in the town of Netanya. In the wake of that Pesach seder massacre, Israeli forces did reenter the West Bank. But if you visit Jenin tomorrow-I don't recommend that you do, by the way-but if you visit Jenin tomorrow you'll see that Jenin was never touched at all, let alone razed during that time. The charge that the IDF razed the town was widely circulated at the time but had no basis in fact. In the past, canards existed, but they existed chiefly at the margins. They didn't appear in scholarly books published by Princeton University Press. The new wrinkle, in this rather old and dismal subject, is a movement of hostility that used to be regarded as disreputable into the mainstream — a hostility that calls itself "criticism of Israel" but is better identified as "anti-Zionism" and , in its most blatant examples, resembles "anti-Semitism."

To give you one more example of how far into the mainstream it goes, have a look, if your scruples will allow you, at the October, 2007 number of *Playboy magazine.* It includes an article called, "Israel Shouldn't Get a Free Pass." Its subtitle is "Real Debate is Not Anti-Semitic."

According to Jacqueline Rose, in her Princeton Press book, there was a time when low and behold, Adolph Hitler and Theodore Herzl attended the Paris Opera House for an opera written by Wagner. Herzl died in 1904, Hitler never stepped foot in Paris before 1940.

Now, I don't know any one who would say real debate is anti-Semitic. The author of this article is Jonathan Tasini. In 2006 he ran for office in the New York state Democratic senatorial primary. He lost. Jonathan Tasini insists that "real debate is not anti-Semitic." He is right, of course, but, then, no serious person claims that real debate is Anti-Semitic. To suggest that it is is to fabricate. After making this ploy, Tasini declares himself to be for "peace, justice, and human rights." Of course. There's no one in this room who is not for peace, justice and human rights. But where does this righteous posture take him? It takes him to Jimmy Carter's book, *Palestine: Peace Not Apartheid.* He praises the book and goes on to say that in the United States it's impossible to be critical of Israel without being labeled "antisemitic or worse." I'm not sure what, by the way, is worse than being labeled "anti-Semitic." It's a severely heavy charge and one should not make it lightly. But the notion that we cannot have honest, legitimate, open debate in America that's critical of Israel, is nothing more than standard fare in "criticism of Israel." In short, it's a phony charge, now routinely pulled out of the rhetorical tool-box employed by those who are given to expressing hostility to Israel and the Jews.

Two more examples. I brought with me one of many books I now have in my collection of hateful books about Israel. This work is called, *Israel: Opposing Views.* On the cover is a graphic illustration of Israel showing the Israeli flag. And, since this book is called Israel: Opposing Views, the opposing view is also graphically represented. How so? If you look hard at the picture you'll see people wearing combat boots stamping on the flag of Israel. Is it conceivable to you-it's not to me-that any Israeli soldier in uniform would step on the Israeli flag? It would just never happen. So, some one-not an Israeli soldier-is stepping on the Israeli flag. Hence, we have Israel and an "opposing view" of Israel, one that desecrates the very idea of Israel as a Jewish nation-state.

This books' publisher is Gale Thompson, one of this country's mainline publishers of school texts. I imagine-I don't know for sure-I imagine this is probably pegged at either the upper middle school level or the high school level. The table of contents shows the first chapter, which has six sub-sections, titled: "Should Israel exist?" Can you imagine that question being asked about any other country on Earth? Should Israel exist?

In Yiddish we call this a "klotzkashe"—a dumb question. One doesn't ask such a question in order to search out a real answer. Nor does the question—"Should Israel exist?"—intend to provoke valid criticism, to get real debate going. Should Canada exist? Should Brazil exist? Should Saudi Arabia exist? Should Japan exist? No one would ask those questions. And for good reason: these countries already do exist, as does Israel, and their legitimacy, like Israel's legitimacy, should not be called into question. And yet, in the very opening chapter of this book, school children are encouraged to discuss: "should Israel exist?" Is this a merely "dumb" question or a mischievous one? Consider how the editors of the book not only frame it but present a range of possibilities for the school children to answer it. The first sub-section under this heading is called "Israel has a right to exist." Thank you. And the second one, the opposing view, is "Israel has no right to exist." The author is Rabbi Avraham Cohen. Rabbi Cohen was one of the featured speakers at Iranian President Mahmoud Ahmadinejad's conference on Holocaust denial last year. He is not, of course, identified in this way in the book. So, American school children can now debate the question of Israel's right to exist , answering, if they wish, in the negative, their answer carrying the approval of a rabbi, to be sure a Neturei Karta rabbi, but a rabbi nonetheless. The school children won't know what Neturei Karta is, but with Rabbi Cohen's hechsher they can now forthrightly debate: Should Israel exist?

There is another chapter, "Should Israel Remain a Jewish State?" It , too, offers answers pro and con. The con comes to us from Joel Kovel, a distinguished pro-

In the opening chapter of the book, *Israel: Opposing Views,* what school children are to discuss is "should Israel exist?"

fessor at Bard College, in New York. Professor Kovel, too, opposes Israel's right to continued existence as a Jewish state. But instead of citing his words as they appear in Israel; Opposing Views, I will cite some words from his recently published book, *Overcoming Zionism: Creating a Single Democratic State in Israel/ Palestine.*

Succinctly put, Professor Kovel's vision of Israel is that there should be no Israel. It should be replaced by a new state to be called "Palisrael." This notion comes to a point of culmination in a series of ten theses set forth in the book's penultimate chapter. In the interest of time, I'm going to read to you only the titles of theses 7, 8, 9, 10.

Professor Joel Kovel

Number 7: A racist state is absolutely illegitimate. Here he is correct. A racist state is absolutely illegitimate. If it is possible to demonstrate that a state, any state, is inherently, structurally, implacably racist, then it does not have legitimacy and does not deserve to continue.

Number 8: Israel as a Jewish State is a racist state. Alex and Andrea address this charge in their own presentations and refute it definitively, so I'll simply refer you to them to disprove this kind of malevolence.

Number 9: Quoting Professor Kovel, "the problem then is Zionism itself" and the Jewish state as such. It's not what he calls "this illegal occupation of the West Bank," but the existence of the Jewish state as such that is the "problem." How, then, to solve this "problem?" the answer is given unambiguously in the following thesis.

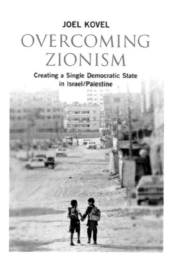

JOEL KOVEL

OVERCOMING ZIONISM

Creating a Single Democratic State in Israel/Palestine

Thesis number 10: Israel does not have the right to exist. We shouldn't be surprised by that conclusion. If left unchecked, the momentum of hostility to Israel now underway almost inevitably leads there. What, then, to do? I will close by once again citing Denis MacShane, with whose admonitory words this lecture began. This is what Mr. MacShane concludes: "We are at the beginning of a long intellectual and ideological struggle. It's not about Jews or Israel. It is about everything democrats have fought for: the truth without fear, no matter one's religion or political beliefs. The new anti-Semitism threatens all of humanity. The Jew-haters must not pass." I would only add: the Jewish Jew-haters also must not pass.

The Motives of Israel's Jewish Defamers

by Kenneth Levin

To the extent that the panel this afternoon is focused generally on Jews who attack the legitimacy of Zionism, or Israel's right to exist as a Jewish state, or compare Israel to the most execrable of states, including Nazi Germany, we are only touching on the extreme of a range of defamation that takes many other forms.

Amos Elon

For example, Amos Elon, long perhaps Israel's most prominent political essayist and not one who has called for the dissolution of Israel or claimed its creation was illegitimate, nevertheless has repeatedly made false accusations against the state. To cite but one instance, in an article about a visit to Amman in 1994, Elon wrote that in recent decades Jordan had forged ahead in all areas, including education and health care, while the West Bank and Gaza had stagnated under Israeli control.

But in fact the opposite was true. According to the United Nations and others, the population of the territories had fared much better with regard both to education and health care than had Jordanians. Adult literacy had progressed further in the territories than in Jordan, and such basic measures of health care as infant mortality and life expectancy yielded dramatically greater improvement in the West Bank and Gaza than in Jordan. The issue is not Elon's being critical of Israel's policies in the territories; it is his defaming Israel by claiming it unconscionably undermined Palestinian health care and education.

> **Besiegement is a psychologically unpleasant condition, and almost invariably under such circumstances, part of the besieged population will embrace the perspectives of the attackers, however bigoted and absurd, in the hope of thereby escaping its predicament.**

But the "motivation" to defame a community with which one has a national or ethnic or religious or other connection is not too difficult to fathom when that community happens to be under chronic attack. Besiegement is a psychologically unpleasant condition, and almost invariably under such circumstances, part of the besieged population will embrace the perspectives of the attackers, however bigoted and absurd, in the hope of thereby escaping its predicament.

Those who do so may seek to reform their community in a manner consistent with the haters' indictments, nurturing the wish that the community will thereby appease the besiegers and end the enmity. Or, they may seek to separate what they identify as their own part of the community from the rest, perhaps from those on the other side of social or political or religious divides; may choose to construe other segments as fitting the besiegers' indictments and seek to exempt their own branch of the community from assault. Or they may simply abandon what they have come to see as a tainted identity. Finally, they may join the attackers as a means of more thoroughly separating themselves from their status as target.

All of these tacks have been taken by some Jews under the duress that was typically part of the Jewish predicament over the millennia of the Diaspora, and they have all also been taken by some Jews in response to the chronic Arab besiegement of Israel.

In the Diaspora beginning with early modernity, over the last two hundred years, every claim raised in Europe against extending civic rights to Jews had its Jewish supporters.

For example, in the Diaspora beginning with early modernity, over the last two hundred years, every claim raised in Europe against extending civic rights to Jews had its Jewish supporters. When it was said that Jews were overwhelmingly occupied with trade and this was itself degenerate and demonstrated their not being fit for civic equality, there were many Jewish voices that agreed and said Jews had to leave their current occupations and become farmers to render themselves fit to be accepted by their neighbors.

And when some in the wider society argued that Yiddish was a degenerate language and was further evidence of Jews being inappropriate candidates for equality, some Jews insisted that their co-religionists must give up Yiddish—not simply because adopting the normative language of the surrounding society would be pragmatic, but because, they agreed, Yiddish is intrinsically degenerate and inferior and rendered Jews unsuitable for acceptance as equals.

As to segments of the community blaming other segments for the Jews' besiegement, one had, for example, in the nineteenth century and beyond, German Jews blaming eastern European Jews for anti-Semitism, and secular or reformist Jews blaming the traditionally religious, and socialist Jews blaming the Jewish middle class, the Jewish bourgeoisie.

And, of course, there were those who simply abandoned the community to escape the taint of being Jewish. Finally there were those who chose to join the Jews' attackers, to separate themselves even more thoroughly from the taint. Such figures joined attackers across the political spectrum. The convert Friedrich Stahl (1802-1861) became professor of ecclesiastic law at the University of Berlin and head of the anti-Jewish Christian Conservative Party; and on the Left one has, of course, Karl Marx and his anti-Jewish ravings, along with many others.

The same pattern can be seen in the Jewish response to the Arab siege of Israel. Some have embraced the indictments of Israel by its enemies, however bigoted or absurd, and have sought to reform Israel to address those indictments in the hope of thereby appeasing the state's enemies.

The same pattern can be seen in the Jewish response to the Arab siege of Israel. Some have embraced the indictments of Israel by its enemies, however bigoted or absurd, and have sought to reform Israel to address those indictments in the hope of thereby appeasing the state's enemies. This can range from insisting— despite all the evidence to the contrary—that Israel's presence in the territories is the cause of Arab enmity and withdrawal to the pre-1967 lines will bring peace; to the argument that Israel's very existence is illegitimate and peace can only come with de-Zionization or de-Judaization or dismantling of the state.

Then there are those who argue that the source of the problem is some other part of the community and insist they themselves should not be seen to share their taint. In Israel, we see this in the claim of many on the Left that the right-wing parties are the obstacles to peace because they have stood in the way of the state making the territorial and other concessions that supposedly would end the siege. In the Diaspora, we see this division most strikingly in those who argue that the proper Jewish path is a focus on international humanitarian issues, that their Judaism has nothing to do with narrow, nationalist concerns, and so they and those who think as they do should be exempted from the taint that attaches to Israel for its alleged crimes.

Then there are people who have responded to the siege by separating themselves from Israel and perhaps from all things Jewish.

And finally there are those who join the besiegers. Among them are both Jews who are active in Jewish communal affairs and those who are not, whose only open affiliation with matters Jewish seems to be as attackers of Israel.

Again, there is a huge range of defamers of Israel. Those who, in response to the siege, challenge the legitimacy of the state are only the most extreme.

In Israel itself, the cultural and academic elites have been particularly prolific in generating defamation of the state, including attacks on its legitimacy. Within Israeli academia, attacking Israel's legitimacy has become virtually a paradigm of interdisciplinary cooperation, attracting people from myriad disciplines.

The academic assault on the state has a pedigree that goes back to the Yishuv, the Jewish community in Mandate Palestine, and to the Diaspora: Among the arguments raised in central Europe against granting civic rights to Jews was that the Jews were a separate, alien nation. In reaction, many Jews sought to demonstrate that they were exclusively a community of faith, not a nation. German-Jewish reformist movements in the early nineteenth century even sought to change the liturgy to delete references to longing for Eretz Israel and Jerusalem in order to erase any suggestions of national, and not purely religious, Jewish identity and aspirations.

Elements of the German Jewish community in the Yishuv embraced these same predilections and defined the proper Zionist project as the building of a Jewish cultural center, not a state, in Eretz Israel. With that mind-set, they responded to Arab attacks during the Mandate in a manner similar to how so many of them had reacted to anti-Jewish indictments in Europe: They even more emphatically argued against nation-building, justified Arab aggression as a reasonable response to the misguided state-building of the Yishuv leadership, and viciously criticized Ben-Gurion and his pro-state associates.

Of course, they did not acknowledge that they were seeking to placate the Jews' attackers but rather wrapped their stance in moral self-righteousness. They insisted—like their present day acolytes—that Judaism had evolved be-

Martin Buber

yond narrow, nationalist concerns, had become exclusively focused on its universal message and mission as a moral force in the world, and that nation-building represented a regressive, atavistic and shameful direction for Jews.

The most prominent figure in this camp was the famous German Jewish philosopher Martin Buber. Even as Jews were desperate to get out of Europe in the late 1930's, Buber and his circle at Hebrew University (Buber himself arrived in the Yishuv in 1938) opposed liberalizing Jewish immigration as serving the cause of state-building, supported British limits on immigration, including those of the notorious Chamberlain White Paper of 1939, and insisted there be no additional immigration without Arab consent.

In an article in *Ha'aretz* in November, 1939, two months after the start of World War II, Buber argued not only that the Zionist objective of a state was immoral but that Zionism was "performing the acts of Hitler in the land of Israel, for they [i.e., the Zionists] want to serve Hitler's god [i.e., nationalism] after he has been given a Hebrew name."

Among more recent Israeli academics, Moshe Zimmermann, a historian at Hebrew University, has argued that there is no such thing as a Jewish people or Jewish nation with its own distinctive history but rather separate communities that had more in common with the larger societies amid which they resided, and so the entire premise of Zionism, as representing the aspirations of the Jewish people and a solution to the difficulties that have dogged and ravaged the Jewish nation, is based on a lie.

Of course, Zimmermann's arguments are vulnerable to myriad rebuttals. The idea that Jewish communities shared much with their local societies is hardly a retort to their sharing values and aspirations with each other as well, or hardly negates historical truths of shared vulnerability and victimization. And, in any case, the identification with Zion and immigration to Israel were not something imposed on Diaspora Jews by Zionist myth-makers but were chosen by Jews, at times under the pressure of external tormentors but still chosen. It is those who would deprive Jews of that choice who could more properly be seen as the culpable ideologues.

Moshe Zimmerman

Even as Jews were desperate to get out of Europe in the late 1930's, Buber and his circle at Hebrew University (Buber himself arrived in the Yishuv in 1938) opposed liberalizing Jewish immigration as serving the cause of state-building, supported British limits on immigration, including those of the notorious Chamberlain White Paper of 1939, and insisted there be no additional immigration without Arab consent.

Moreover, virtually all modern nation-states, for example Britain and France as well as Israel, were created by the amalgamation of populations diverse in important ways, and typically by coercion being an important part of the mix, unlike in Israel's history. To argue that the disparate cultural strands of the Israeli Jewish population somehow delegitimizes the Zionist enterprise or the state is itself a narrow anti-Jewish bias. Indeed Zimmermann's is an anti-Jewish bias of a particularly crude sort, as when he compares Israeli public school education in Israeli history and Zionism not to education in national history and national culture in Britain or France or the United States, but to the education of Hitler Youth.

Zimmermann's work explicitly connects historical revisionism with the advancement of a post-Zionist agenda. According to Zimmermann, as there was no Jewish nation or people to provide a foundation for a legitimate national liberation movement, Zionism is bogus and, in any case, passe, and so it ought to be discarded into the trashbin of history.

Joseph Agassi, a professor of philosophy at Tel Aviv University, has similarly written that Israel, having established itself on the basis of a misconceived "phantom nation" (i.e., the Jewish people), is consequently similar to the Soviet Union and—as you may well have guessed—Nazi Germany.

The writings of some other academics during this time focus less on details of the alleged misbegetting of Zionism and simply emphasize Zionism's sinfulness or, at best, its obsolescence. Menahem Brinker, a professor of Hebrew literature at Hebrew University, declared in a *Jerusalem Post* article in September, 1995, that Zionism is a "totalitarian" concept that "has outlived its usefulness and will ebb away in time."

Professor Moshe Zimmermann's is an anti-Jewish bias of a particularly crude sort, as when he compares Israeli public school education in Israeli history and Zionism not to education in national history and national culture in Britain or France or the United States, but to the education of Hitler Youth.

Another front in Israel in the effort to delegitimize Israel and the concept of a Jewish state has involved attacks on the Jewish nature of such symbols of the state as the flag and the national anthem, Hatikvah; and, most notably, attacks on the Law of Return.

Israel enacted the Law of Return, actually two laws, almost at the very inception of the state, giving Jews everywhere the right to come to Israel (1950) and attain immediate citizenship (1952). Among anti-Zionist and post-Zionist groups the criticism has been particularly that the Law of Return is racist and undemocratic, and this theme was advanced with growing intensity during the early 1990's.

For example, an article by Ran Kislev in *Ha'aretz* in July, 1990, called the Law of Return "reminiscent of the Nuremberg Laws." Another by Danny Rubinstein (July, 1991) declared it the kind of discrimination that "was the basis for the apartheid regime in South Africa." This is the same Danny Rubinstein that, as Andrea Levin has mentioned, insisted, at the recent UN anti-Israel conference held at the European parliament in Brussels, that Israel is an apartheid state.

David Grossman

Historian Tom Segev (October, 1995) maintained that the Law of Return "contradicts the essence of democracy."

Novelist David Grossman (in *Yediot Aharonot,* September 29, 1993) insisted the Law of Return is an obstacle to "full equality" for Israeli Arabs. Yuli Tamir, then on the philosophy faculty of Tel Aviv University and currently Israel's minister of education, argued that the Law of Return constitutes "a violation of the right of national minorities to equal treatment."

Alvin Rosenfeld, in the reaction to his American Jewish Committee monograph, has been accused of attacking all so-called "progressives" and trying to silence any criticism of Israel. But, of course, he is discussing not those who simply criticize some Israeli policies but those who defame Israel, more specifically those who defame her in the most extreme, bigoted manner. There are, in fact, people who by virtually any criteria are within the "progressive" camp and yet share Alvin's perspective.

Amnon Rubinstein is a former dean of the law school at Tel Aviv University, long a member of the Meretz Party, which is of course to the left of Labor, and was for a time Minister of Education in the Labor-Meretz coalition government that oversaw the first three years of the Oslo process. Despite his being critical of various Israeli policies prior to Oslo, he has vehemently condemned those other critics who defame the state, and not only where that defamation has sunk to the level of delegitimizing Israel.

For example, the New Historians are a group of Israeli historians who emerged mainly in the late 1980's offering a largely bogus rewriting of Israel's past, particularly concerning the War of Independence but also touching on the Mandate years as well as the years immediately after the 1947-48 war. The common thread of the New Historians is criticism of Jewish policies and charging those policies with bearing much of the responsibility for Palestinian and broader Arab enmity. The subtext of the New History, stated at times explicitly by its authors, is that if only Israelis would recognize their culpability and make sufficient amends, then the way to peace would be open.

The New Historians' attitudes toward the state vary widely—from Benny Morris, who, for all his defamatory distortion of events in that earlier period, certainly has not advocated the dissolution of Israel, to Ilan Pappe, who, in various forms, has advocated precisely that.

Amnon Rubinstein has been a harsh critic of the entire spectrum of New Historians. He has argued that, contrary to their claims, the leaders of the Yishuv made

The subtext of the New History, stated at times explicitly by its authors, is that if only Israelis would recognize their culpability and make sufficient amends, then the way to peace would be open.

all sorts of efforts to reach some accommodation with the Arab population in the pre-state years but were met only with rejection and violence, and that this pattern continued after statehood. Rubinstein also has written of Britain's betrayal of its formal obligations to the Jews during the Mandate, in contrast to the New Historians' inclination to ignore British malfeasance and whitewash British policies.

Rubinstein is critical as well of the post-Zionist academics, pointing out the intellectual dishonesty that is characteristic of their arguments. He notes the predilection of many post-Zionists and new historians to criticize the concept of objective history and talk of competing narratives. But, he observes, they then dismiss the Jewish narrative and accord legitimacy only to the Arab version of truth, while typically omitting information that might cast a negative light on the Palestinians and other Arabs. Rubinstein refers also to their inclination to judge Israel by an impossible standard that no polity could meet.

Speaking more broadly of fellow left-leaning Israelis, Rubinstein has stated they have had difficulty coping with the animosity directed against them as Israelis and Jews, confronted as they are not only with Arab hostility but also the bigoted animosity to which they are subjected in the United Nations, in Europe, and elsewhere. He has suggested that this has driven them to close their eyes to the truth of Arab hatred and intransigence and to embrace as reality fantasies of a benign Levant that does not exist.

Rubinstein's dedication to assuring equal rights for Israel's minorities has been steadfast and a central tenet of his political agenda. But he has observed, with regard to post-Zionist attacks on the flag and Hatikvah, that flags and national anthems are typically rooted in a national and religious tradition. He has argued that "this connection seems to be conventionally accepted even in the most enlightened countries—countries where Jews live under flags adorned with crosses without feeling that their rights have been compromised."

With regard to the Law of Return, he has noted the obvious hypocrisy of those who condemn it as racist and unfair to Israel's Arab minority while at the same time putting forward, as models for Israel, certain European democracies. Yet many of these countries themselves give immigration and citizenship preference to those with ethnic ties to the majority group in their states, do so without these groups having the horrific histories of forced exile and persecution that the Jews do, and obviously do so without regarding the relevant policies and laws as undemocratic. These states include, for example, Denmark, Italy, Greece, and Ireland.

Amnon Rubinstein

> **With regard to the Law of Return, Amnon Rubinstein has noted the obvious hypocrisy of those who condemn it as racist and unfair to Israel's Arab minority while at the same time putting forward, as models for Israel, certain European democracies. Yet many of these countries themselves give immigration and citizenship preference to those with ethnic ties to the majority group in their states.**

Rubinstein writes at one point, referring to German policy,

> In spite of the existence of the European Convention on Human Rights and the European Court for Human Rights, Germany has never been called upon to annul its own 'Law of Return' on grounds that it harms the universal principle of equality... [Moreover,] the right of a state to differentiate between groups of potential immigrants and citizens was expressly recognized in the United Nations Convention on the Elimination of All Forms of Racial Discrimination, ratified in 1965.

In addition, the legitimacy of state policies of preferential repatriation was affirmed by the Council of Europe in 2001.

Again, Rubinstein is critical not only of defamation in the service of delegitimizing Zionism and the Jewish state, but also defamation by those who share his political views, defamation in the course of advocating particular Israeli concessions as the path to peace.

He is critical of the entire range of defamation largely because he recognizes that whether it is calling Israel a Nazi-like, illegitimate entity, the greatest threat to world peace, or it is making false assertions against the state to promote Israeli concessions, all defamation is not simply an assault on intellectual honesty and integrity but serves the cause of those who want to delegitimize and destroy the Jewish state; all defamation of Israel contributes to that hateful, evil end.

The *London* and *New York Review of Books*—Nonsense Masquerading as Sophistication

by Alex Safian

The *New York Review of Books* has been termed the "premier literary-intellectual magazine in the English language," and similarly effusive praise has been directed towards its British derivative, *The London Review of Books*. Among so-called elite journals of opinion, the two hold a special place.

Both feature lengthy essays on a vast array of diverse topics, and both reserve a special animus for Israel and its supporters. Both are, therefore, also the venue of choice for some of Israel's worst Jewish defamers, such as Henry Siegman, Yitzhak Laor, Jacqueline Rose, Tony Judt, Avi Shlaim, Ilan Pappe, and also some of Israel's worst non-Jewish defamers, like Stephen Walt and John Mearsheimer, whose article on the Israel lobby first appeared in the *London Review*.

Not surprisingly, the staffs of both journals are also heavily Jewish. For example, Mary-Kay Wilmers, the editor of the *London Review,* has cited her own Jewish heritage when her magazine's articles provoke glee from anti-Semites. Here is how she responded when neo-Nazi and former KKK leader David Duke warmly embraced the Walt/Mearsheimer article:

> I don't want David Duke to endorse the article. It makes me feel uncomfortable. But when I re-read the piece, I did not see anything that I felt should not have been said. Maybe it is because I am Jewish, but I think I am very alert to anti-Semitism. And I do not think that criticising US foreign policy, or Israel's way of going about influencing it, is anti-Semitic. I just don't see it.

One can certainly see why she's been termed the "materfamilias of London's liberal intelligentsia." Similarly, the legendary Robert Silvers, co-founder and editor of the *New York Review,* is also Jewish.

Now, for those who don't regularly read these journals, I'd like to give you a flavor of the sort of refined, high-minded intellectualism that so often graces their pages. These words by Mary Beard, Classics Professor at Cambridge, were published in the *London Review* just after 9/11:

> But when the shock had faded, more hard-headed reaction set in. This wasn't just the feeling that, however tactfully you dress it up, the United States had it coming. That is, of course, what many people openly or privately think. World bullies, even if their heart is in the right place, will in the end pay the price.

When Mary Beard says that "many people" think we had it coming, it reminds

The *London* and *New York Review of Books* are, therefore, also the venue of choice for some of Israel's worst Jewish defamers, such as Henry Siegman, Yitzhak Laor, Jacqueline Rose, Tony Judt, Avi Shlaim, Ilan Pappe.

me of the oft-cited reaction by *New York Times* critic Pauline Kael to Richard Nixon's victory in 1972—"How could Nixon have won? Nobody I know voted for him." In other words, it depends on your circle of friends, and I guess we now know what we need to about Mary Beard's circle of friends.

Still, so much for the claim that the United States squandered the goodwill of the world after 9/11. Apparently, in certain tweedy corners, there was little goodwill to squander. Professor Beard also reassured her readers that there was little henceforth to worry about, since suicide terrorists, what she calls martyrs, are so rare:

> But almost the oddest response has been our terrified certainty that there remains a plentiful supply of suicide pilots and bombers. Anyone who has scratched the surface of early Christianity will realise that full-blown martyrs are a rare commodity, much more numerous in the imagination than on the ground.

Only someone getting her news from the BBC or the *Guardian*—and who therefore missed so many of the pre-9/11 suicide bombings in Israel—could possibly say so ridiculous a thing. And perhaps in referring to early Christianity the good professor is scratching the surface of the wrong religion.

Ignoring Palestinian suicide bombings and the Palestinian hate education that has fueled these bombings and made peace impossible, and generally ignoring facts and twisting facts, is a common occurrence at these journals, the better to put Israel alone in the dock and under the microscope.

A prime example of this unfortunate phenomenon is Henry Siegman, former head of the American Jewish Congress and former member of the Council on Foreign Relations.

Siegman's work is emblematic of Israel's Jewish defamers, and his technique is on full display in a *London Review* article from August 16, titled "Great Middle East Peace Process Scam."

In the article Siegman claims that:

> The Middle East peace process may well be the most spectacular deception in modern diplomatic history. Since the failed Camp David summit of 2000, and actually well before it, Israel's interest in a peace process—other than for the purpose of obtaining Palestinian and international acceptance of the status quo—has been a fiction that has served primarily to provide cover for its systematic confiscation of Palestinian land and an occupation whose goal, according to the former IDF chief of staff Moshe Ya'alon, is 'to sear deep into the consciousness of Palestinians that they are a defeated people.'

Now, it is a strange strategy indeed that aims to confiscate land first by reaching an agreement with the Palestine Liberation Organization, and then by turning

Ignoring Palestinian suicide bombings and the Palestinian hate education that has fueled these bombings and made peace impossible, and generally ignoring facts and twisting facts, is a common occurrence at these journals, the better to put Israel alone in the dock and under the microscope.

that land over to a newly-created Palestinian Authority—the PLO by another name. And then by assisting in the formation of armed Palestinian militias manned largely by "former" PLO terrorists who are allowed in by Israel, and then by basing them within walking distance of Israeli cities. Not to mention trusting Yasir Arafat's promises for a "peace of the brave" and a crackdown on terrorists, and thus inviting him, too, back into the region.

Of course, Siegman is entitled to his opinions, no matter how bizarre. But what about the facts he uses to support his opinions? What about that alleged quote by Moshe Ya'alon? Did General Ya'alon really say, as Siegman claims, that Israel's goal was to 'to sear deep into the consciousness of Palestinian Arabs that they are a defeated people'?

Siegman gives no references for this, and searches on the exact phrase just refer back to Siegman's article. But a google search on key parts of the supposed Ya'alon quote is more enlightening. It turns out that Rashid Khalidi has an almost identical quote attributed to Ya'alon in his book Resurrecting Empire:

> The Palestinians must be made to understand in the deepest recesses of their consciousness that they are a defeated people.

Khalidi also has this quote in the body of the chapter, and in a footnote he cites a *Washington Times* column by Arnaud de Borchgrave, and indicates that de Borchgrave got the quote from a specific *Ha'aretz* article by the very good Israeli journalist Ari Shavit.

Now, de Borchgrave does indeed have the quote, but with no clear citation for it. How then does Khalidi know it's from Shavit? Maybe he asked de Borchgrave —but the important question remains, is the Ya'alon quote accurate?

Of course, the answer is no—Ya'alon said nothing of the sort.

The *Ha'aretz* article in question, published on Aug. 30, 2002, is a memorable, very lengthy interview of Ya'alon, notable for the depth of Shavit's questions and the candor of Ya'alon's answers.

Here then is what Ya'alon actually said about the consciousness of Palestinians.

Moshe Ya'alon

First the question by Shavit, followed by Ya'alon's answer:

> Do you have a definition of victory? Is it clear to you what Israel's goal in this war is?

> I defined it from the beginning of the confrontation: the very deep internalization by the Palestinians that terrorism and violence will not defeat us, will not make us fold. If that deep internalization does not exist at the end of the confrontation, we will have a strategic problem with an existential threat to Israel. If that [lesson] is not burned into the Palestinian and Arab consciousness, there will be no end to their demands of us. Despite our military might, the region will perceive us as being even weaker. That will have an impact not only on those who are engaged in the violent struggle, but also on those who have signed agreements with us and on extremists among the Arabs in Israel.

In a followup question General Ya'alon repeated the point:

> The facts that are being determined in this confrontation—in terms of what will be burned into the Palestinian consciousness—are fateful. If we end the confrontation in a way that makes it clear to every Palestinian that terrorism does not lead to agreements, that will improve our strategic position. On the other hand, if their feeling at the end of the confrontation is that they can defeat us by means of terrorism, our situation will become more and more difficult.

So Ya'alon said not that the Palestinian Arabs must understand they are a defeated people, but that they must understand that Palestinian terrorism will not make Israelis a defeated people.

The difference between Ya'alon's actual statement and the claims of Khalidi and de Borchgrave and Siegman could not be more stark. The doctored quotation is, in plain terms, a blatant lie.

Did Rashid Khalidi, the Columbia University historian, not check the primary source, the original interview in *Ha'aretz?* Or worse, did he check it, and use the falsified version of the quotation anyhow?

Exactly the same questions must be asked of Siegman and de Borchgrave. Must be asked, and will be asked.

Unfortunately this is not the only phony quotation in Siegman's article. For example, Siegman claims that then Prime Minister Ariel Sharon's senior aide Dov Weissglas revealed in a *Ha'aretz* interview that Sharon's disengagement strategy was really intended to destroy the peace process. In fact, the interview, in Hebrew, shows that Weissglas said more or less the opposite.

Besides falsifying quotations, Siegman also falsifies the meaning of documents like United Nations Security Council Resolution 242, passed in the wake of the Six Day War.

Siegman misleads his readers by claiming that:

> ... implicit in Israel's occupation policy [is] that if no peace agreement is reached, the 'default setting' of UN Security Council Resolution 242 is the indefinite continuation of Israel's occupation. If this reading were true, the resolution would actually be inviting an occupying power that wishes to retain its adversary's territory to do so simply by means of avoiding peace talks - which is exactly what Israel has been doing. In fact, the introductory statement to Resolution 242 declares that territory cannot be acquired by war, implying that if the parties cannot reach agreement, the occupier must withdraw to the status quo ante: that, logically, is 242's default setting.

This is, to say the least, an inventive reading of Resolution 242, as it creates what might be called in international law a "right of do-over." If the Arab countries attack and try to destroy Israel, but fail, the territory they lose in the attempt must be unconditionally returned to them, so they can try again from the same advantageous position. They just rearm, and, like a schoolyard bully, demand a do-over. And, under the Siegman rules, this goes on, presumably, until they finally succeed in destroying Israel.

Now, as it happens, there are other very different interpretations of Resolution 242, especially from the people who actually wrote the resolution. The US Ambassador to the UN at the time, Arthur Goldberg, and his British counterpart, Lord Caradon, who actually introduced the resolution, took the position that Israel was not obligated to unilaterally withdraw, and that any eventual withdrawal would not have to be to the pre-1967 line.

As Ambassador Goldberg put it:

> The notable omissions—which were not accidental—in regard to withdrawal are the words 'the' or 'all' and the 'June 5, 1967 lines' ... the resolution speaks of withdrawal from occupied territories without defining the extent of withdrawal. [This would encompass] less than a complete withdrawal of Israeli forces from occupied territory, inasmuch as Israel's prior frontiers had proved to be notably insecure.

Of course, it should not be ignored that by withdrawing from Sinai, Israel has already withdrawn from 80% of the territories.

And here's how Lord Caradon viewed Resolution 242:

> It would have been wrong to demand that Israel return to its positions of June 4, 1967, because those positions were undesirable and artificial.

During the negotiations over the resolution at the UN one other very important country's representative made a key statement on how to interpret the resolution:

> ... "secure and recognized boundaries". What does that mean? What boundar-

ies are these? Secure, recognized—by whom, for what? Who is going to judge how secure they are? Who must recognize them? ... there is certainly much leeway for different interpretations which retain for Israel the right to establish new boundaries and to withdraw its troops only as far as the lines which it judges convenient.

Who said this? No, it wasn't Abba Eban—it was the Soviet representative, Deputy Foreign Minister Vasily Kuznetsov.

The Soviets didn't like the resolution for precisely this reason, but in the end they voted for it because for them it was more important to stabilize the situation after the war so they could get on with the massive task of rearming and rebuilding the Arab armies. So that the Arab armies could once again be in a position to attack Israel, which, of course, is exactly what happened a few short years later.

In order to make his tendentious arguments, Siegman has to ignore or mangle all this documented history. And he displays what can only be called breathtaking creativity when he argues that Israel should be forced to withdraw not just from the post-1967 line, but from the pre-1967 line:

> In the course of a war launched by Arab countries that sought to prevent the implementation of the UN partition resolution, Israel enlarged its territory by 50 per cent. If it is illegal to acquire territory as a result of war, then the question now cannot conceivably be how much additional Palestinian territory Israel may confiscate, but rather how much of the territory it acquired in the course of the war of 1948 it is allowed to retain. At the very least, if 'adjustments' are to be made to the 1949 armistice line, these should be made on Israel's side of that line, not the Palestinians'.

So he admits the Arabs launched a war—though he delicately says it was to prevent partition, rather than to destroy Israel—but once again the Siegman rules are applied. The only penalty for this illegal Arab act of war accrues to Israel.

There is yet another aspect of the Siegman rules, and that is that Arab terrorism must be almost entirely ignored. The Israeli response to Arab terrorism is put under the microscope, and always removed from any context.

Thus, here is Siegman describing the situation in Gaza, after the complete Israeli withdrawal, and after more than 1800 missiles have been launched from Gaza, aimed at Israeli communities, and after numerous other cross-border attacks, including the attack in which Israeli soldier Gilad Shalit was abducted and two other Israeli soldiers were killed:

> Gaza's situation shows us what these bantustans will look like if their residents do not behave as Israel wants.

It therefore seems Siegman is arguing that Palestinians have a right to behave as violently as they want and there should be no consequences. Israel should just

Siegman is arguing that Palestinians have a right to behave as violently as they want and there should be no consequences. Israel should just accept missiles and rockets fired into its cities and towns, and all other attacks against Israelis—whether civilian or in uniform—wherever they occur.

accept missiles and rockets fired into its cities and towns, and all other attacks against Israelis—whether civilian or in uniform—wherever they occur. Siegman resolutely refuses to hold accountable the Palestinian perpetrators of these attacks.

Siegman, of course, is not alone in this mentality of "blame Israel first and only." New York University Prof. Tony Judt displays exactly the same habit of mind. He charged, for example, in his notorious *New York Review of Books* article "Israel: The Alternative," which termed Israel an anachronism, that:

> with American support, Jerusalem has consistently and blatantly flouted UN resolutions requiring it to withdraw from land seized and occupied in war.

The only relevant Security Council resolution in this regard is Resolution 242, and it does not require that Israel unconditionally withdraw from land. Judt, just like Siegman, totally distorts the resolution. Indeed, Israel is the only country in the Middle East that accepted Resolution 242 from the start and has never flouted it.

Judt also charges that Israel was a major reason for going to war against Saddam's Iraq:

> It is now tacitly conceded by those in a position to know that America's reasons for going to war in Iraq were not necessarily those advertised at the time. For many in the current US administration, a major strategic consideration was the need to destabilize and then reconfigure the Middle East in a manner thought favorable to Israel.

Such charges are silly and ahistorical, as Prof. Martin Kramer has definitively shown in response to Walt and Mearsheimer. However, it is interesting to look at the supporting reference that Judt seems to provide for this charge:

"See the interview with Deputy Secretary of Defense Paul Wolfowitz in the July 2003 issue of *Vanity Fair.*"

The first sign of trouble here is that, if you check *Vanity Fair,* it's not an interview, it's an article by Sam Tanenhaus, titled "Bush's Brain Trust." And what do we find about Israel in that article? Here, from the more than 6,000-word *Vanity Fair* article, is the only reference to the root word Israel:

> George Bush ... yesterday's servant of oil and gas companies is now "the callow instrument of neoconservative ideologues," as The *New York Review of Books* recently put it. Others warn darkly of a "cabal" or "conspiracy" of mostly Jewish "kosher conservatives" who have "hijacked" the government even as they secretly serve the interests of Israel's Likud Party.

This, to NYU Prof. Tony Judt, is apparently proof that Paul Wolfowitz in an interview said we invaded Iraq for Israel.

Tony Judt

In other words, Judt has more in common with Henry Siegman than merely a shared Jewish heritage. There is also a disturbing willingness—even eagerness—to twist and make up facts, all to further the overriding goal of discrediting and defaming not just Israel but also the supporters of Israel.

And, as mentioned, there are Israelis recruited—or volunteering—to this cause as well, and following much the same script. For example, in a book review and essay entitled "Imagined Territories" in the *London Review of Books,* Yonatan Mendel also rewrites history and facts.

He claims, for example, that though Israel's leaders thought settlements were good for security, during the Yom Kippur War in 1973:

> ... the truth is that the army spent the first days of the Syrian assault evacuating settlements in the Golan before it could proceed with military operations.

What exactly would Mendel have his readers believe the Syrians were doing while the Israeli army was supposedly busy with evacuations and therefore unable to proceed with military operations? Did the Syrian's chivalrously say "So sorry chaps, we'll just wait for you to finish evacuating your civilians first"?

The bizarre idea that the IDF was unable to proceed with military operations would be news indeed to Avigdor Kahalani and his legendary 7th Brigade, which, though desperately outnumbered, fought so heroically to hold off an army of Syrian tanks. It would be news to Generals Eitan and Hofi and Peled, who were leading their men in battle from virtually the first moments of the Syrian attack.

Mendel makes many other strange allegations about settlements as well, for instance that:

> They were built with red roofs in order to distinguish them from Palestinian communities and surrounded by pines in order to acidify the soil and make the land unusable for Palestinian shepherds.

Others have charged Israel harmed the environment by cutting down pine forests in order to build settlements in their place; now Israel is being accused of harming the environment by planting pine forests. You just can't win with these people.

And, of course, leave it to those fiendish Israelis to think of "red tile roofs." Who could imagine such a thing? Probably nowhere else in the world do you see red tile roofs.

For Mendel, it's not just with pine trees and red tiles that Israel supposedly wrongs the Palestinians. There is also the issue of water, specifically of hoarding water and allegedly denying it to Palestinians:

> Israel has a great effect above ground on the lives of Palestinians in the West Bank but there is a continuing struggle for control below ground. Eighty per cent of the mountain aquifers supplying Israelis and Palestinians are located under the West Bank. However, 83 per cent of available water is used for the sole benefit of Israeli cities and settlements.

These numbers are partly right, partly nonsense, and completely misleading, for the simple reason that while the aquifers straddle the line between Israel and the West Bank, most of the water stored in the aquifers is beneath pre-1967 Israel. This is due not to any nefarious Jewish plot, but to the laws of gravity causing water to flow downhill.

The West Bank, heading west from its mountain ridges, is higher in elevation than Israel, which descends to sea level on the shores of the Mediterranean. So water that falls on the western side of the West Bank's mountains percolates into the ground, and then flows downhill, under the surface, into Israel. This water collects in aquifers within Israel, and in the early days of the state, before these aquifers were fully tapped, the water emerged in natural springs, most famously at Rosh Hayin.

Because the water was easily available in Israel, where the aquifer is near the surface, Israelis always used the water, before 1967, and even before 1948. In the 1950's for example, before any presence in the West Bank, Israel used 95 percent of the Western Aquifer's water, and 82 percent of the Northeastern Aquifer's water. Today, Israel's share of these aquifers has declined to 83 percent and 80 percent, respectively.

That is, under direct Israeli administration of the West Bank the Palestinian share of these aquifers has actually increased. In addition, every year over 40 MCM (million cubic meters) of water from sources within Israel are piped over the Green Line for Palestinian use in the West Bank. Ramallah, for example, receives over 5 MCM. Israel sends another 4 MCM over its border for Palestinian use in Gaza. Thus, it is the Palestinians who are using Israeli water. And they use it while they are shooting at Israel, which nonetheless, sends it their way.

And not just Palestinians benefit from Israeli water. Under its treaty with Jordan Israel also provides more than 55 MCM annually to the Kingdom. In contrast, we in the United States are not exactly generous with Mexico when it comes to water, despite the very serious water shortages that Mexicans face.

Perhaps no other country in the world, facing the severe water shortages that

Israel does, has shared so much of its water with so many of its neighbors, even unfriendly neighbors. Needless to say, this reality is exactly the reverse of what Mendel would have his readers believe.

Mendel also adds to his theme of the rapacious Israelis seeking to control what is under the ground, turning his attention to the holiest site in Judaism, the Temple Mount. Here is the absolutely remarkable way he describes the situation:

> At Camp David in 2000, when Ehud Barak negotiated the future of the Temple Mount compound with Arafat, Clinton favoured another 'soft' solution, giving Palestinians full sovereignty over the mosques on the Temple Mount, while Israel would have full sovereignty under the ground — an idea based on the assertion that the remains of the Temple lie beneath the Al-Aqsa mosque and the Dome of the Rock. This proposal was rejected out of hand by Arafat and the negotiations ended. Israel was yet again unwilling to deliver full control and persisted in wanting some kind of hold, archaeological or even symbolic.

That is, for Mendel it's a mere "assertion" that the First and Second Temples were on the Temple Mount — in other words, he in effect joins Arafat in denying that the Temples were even there. Recall that when Arafat leveled this denial at Camp David, President Clinton indignantly pulled out his copy of the Scriptures and told Arafat "You're denying my Bible, too."

Mendel, however, blames Israel for being unwilling to deliver to the Palestinians full control over what is to most Jews the holiest site in Judaism. One wonders, why doesn't he blame the Palestinians for being unyielding on their attachment to Haram a Sharif, which is, after all, at best the third holiest site in Islam? And would he blame the Muslims for their attachment to Mecca and their unwillingness to give up control over Mecca? After all, there were Jews in Mecca - and Medina and the Hejaz, and synagogues as well — before there were Muslims.

Would he begrudge Catholics their attachment to the Vatican, or Christians generally an attachment to their holy places in Jerusalem?

One cannot avoid the belief that for Mendel and Judt and Siegman and for so many of Israel's Jewish defamers, it is only the Jews who must not have attachments to place and time, who must not love and inhabit the land, and to whom, alone among the peoples of the world, sovereignty must be denied.

Perhaps their contempt for facts is really a fear that facing facts also means dealing with unpleasant realities, like hatred that cannot be reasoned with, and cannot be appeased or wished away. Their fantasies, after all, are so much more comforting.

One cannot avoid the belief that for Mendel and Judt and Siegman and for so many of Israel's Jewish defamers, it is only the Jews who must not have attachments to place and time, who must not love and inhabit the land, and to whom, alone among the peoples of the world, sovereignty must be denied.